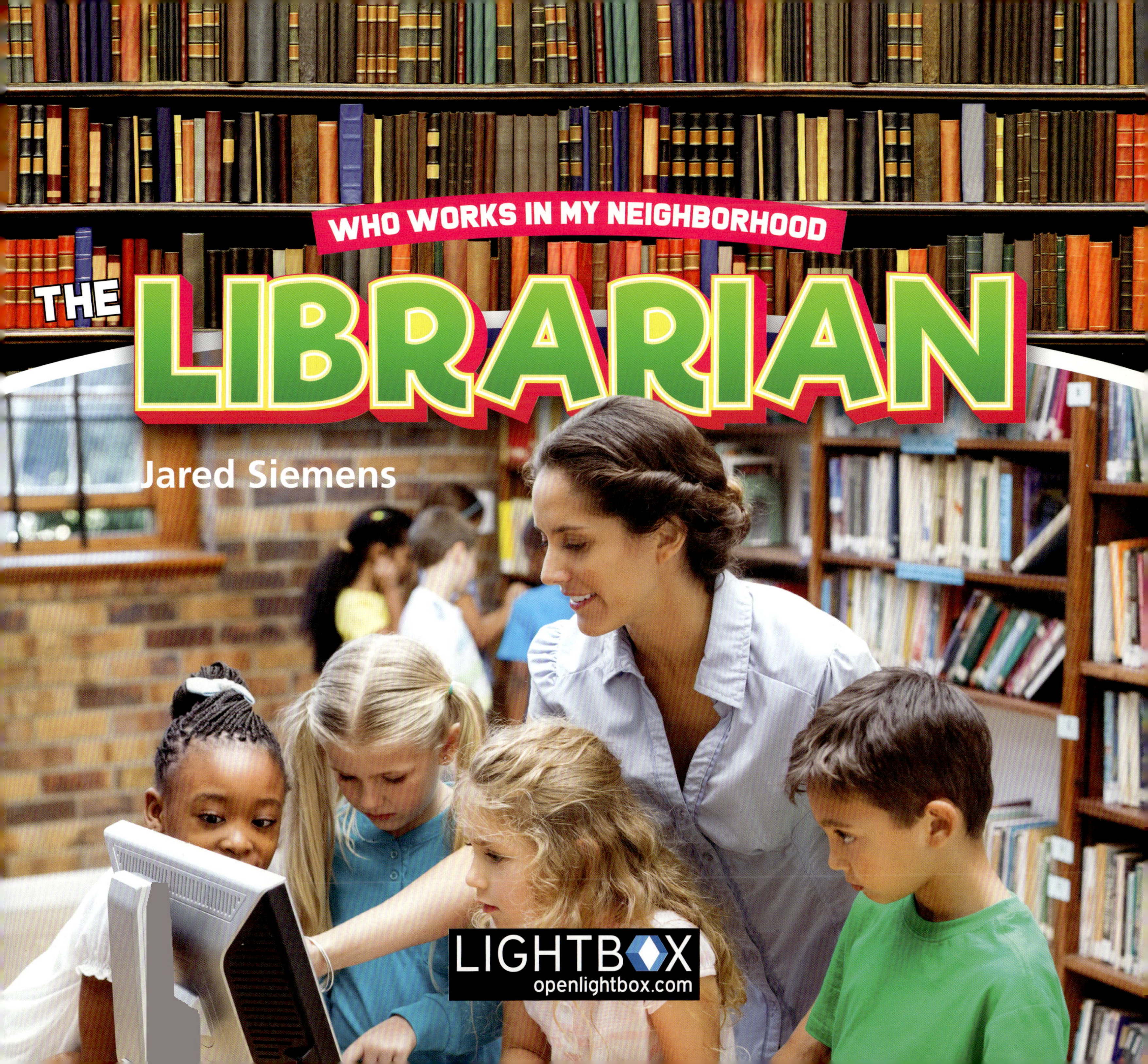
WHO WORKS IN MY NEIGHBORHOOD
THE LIBRARIAN
Jared Siemens
LIGHTBOX
openlightbox.com

Go to
www.openlightbox.com
and enter this book's
unique code.

ACCESS CODE

LBXU3665

Lightbox is an all-inclusive digital solution for the teaching and learning of curriculum topics in an original, groundbreaking way. Lightbox is based on National Curriculum Standards.

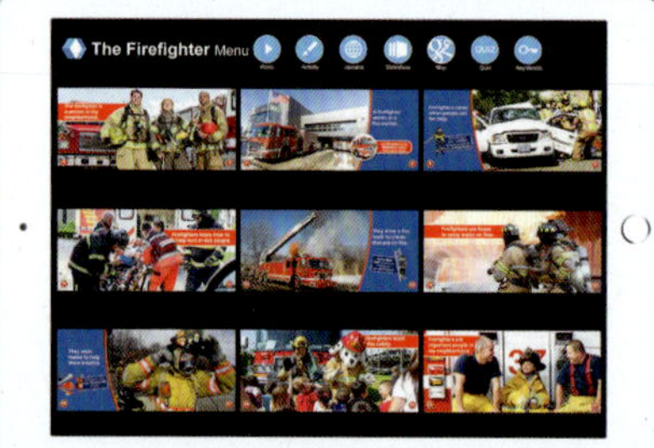

OPTIMIZED FOR

- ✓ **TABLETS**
- ✓ **WHITEBOARDS**
- ✓ **COMPUTERS**
- ✓ **AND MUCH MORE!**

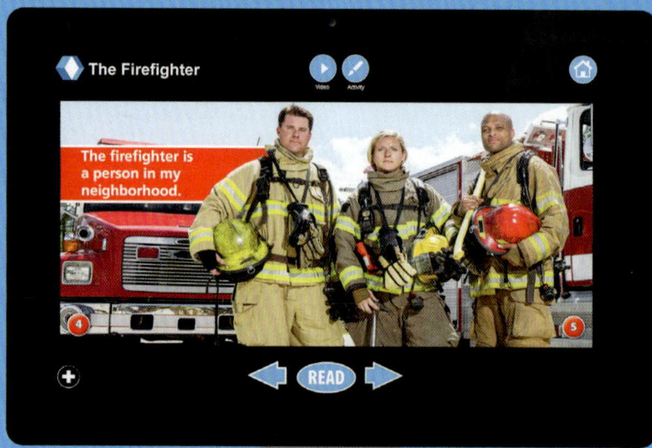

STANDARD FEATURES OF LIGHTBOX

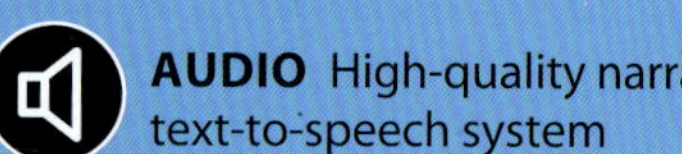
AUDIO High-quality narration using text-to-speech system

VIDEOS Embedded high-definition video clips

ACTIVITIES Printable PDFs that can be emailed and graded

WEBLINKS Curated links to external, child-safe resources

SLIDESHOWS Pictorial overviews of key concepts

INTERACTIVE MAPS Interactive maps and aerial satellite imagery

QUIZZES Ten multiple choice questions that are automatically graded and emailed for teacher assessment

KEY WORDS Matching key concepts to their definitions

VIDEOS

WEBLINKS

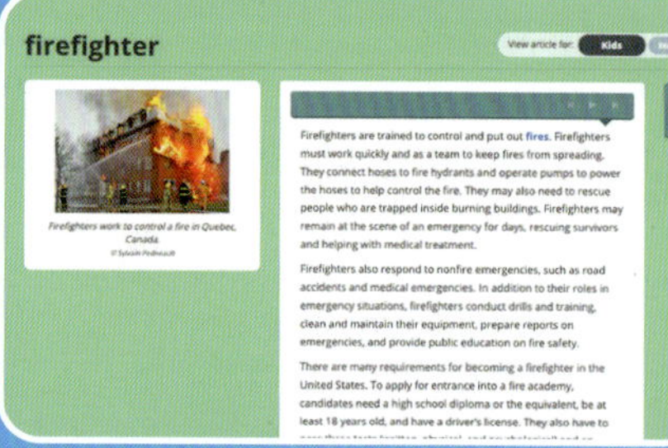

SLIDESHOWS

QUIZZES

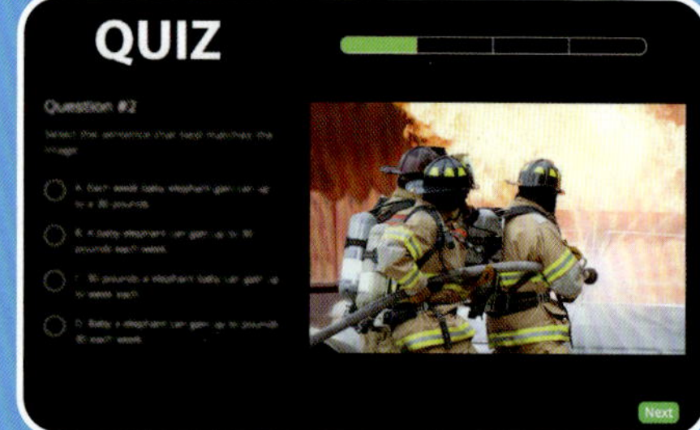

WHO WORKS IN MY NEIGHBORHOOD

THE LIBRARIAN

Contents

The librarian is a person in my neighborhood.

A librarian works in a library.

The **Library of Congress** in Washington, DC, is the **largest** library in the **world**.

The librarian takes care of the library and everything in it.

The librarian helps me find and borrow books.

The **average** person reads about **12 books** each year.

Librarians use computers to help find information.

The **United States** has more than **16,000** public libraries.

The librarian teaches me how to use the internet safely.

The librarian picks new books for the library and makes them easy to find.

The librarian reads books out loud during story time.

Librarians are important people in my neighborhood.

More than **166,000 librarians** work in the United States.

See what you have learned about the librarian.

Describe what you see in each of the pictures.

KEY WORDS

Research has shown that as much as 65 percent of all written material published in English is made up of 300 words. These 300 words cannot be taught using pictures or learned by sounding them out. They must be recognized by sight. This book contains 36 common sight words to help young readers improve their reading fluency and comprehension. This book also teaches young readers several important content words, such as proper nouns. These words are paired with pictures to aid in learning and improve understanding.

Page	Sight Words First Appearance
4	a, in, is, my, the
7	has, miles, more, of, than, works
8	and, it, takes
10	about, books, each, find, helps, me, reads, year
13	states, to, use
14	how
16	for, makes, new, them
19	out, story, time
20	are, important, people

Page	Content Words First Appearance
4	librarian, neighborhood, person
7	bookshelves, library, Library of Congress, Washington, DC
10	borrow
13	computers, information, United States
14	internet

Published by Smartbook Media Inc.
350 5th Avenue, 59th Floor, New York, NY 10118
Website: www.openlightbox.com

Library of Congress Control Number: 2020934517

ISBN 978-1-5105-5355-2 (hardcover)
ISBN 978-1-5105-5356-9 (multi-user eBook)

Printed in Guangzhou, China
1 2 3 4 5 6 7 8 9 0 24 23 22 21 20

042020
110819

Project Coordinator: Ryan Smith
Designer: Ana María Vidal

Every reasonable effort has been made to trace ownership and to obtain permission to reprint copyright material. The publisher would be pleased to have any errors or omissions brought to its attention so that they may be corrected in subsequent printings.

The publisher acknowledges Getty Images, and iStock as the primary image suppliers for this title.